FARTING FISH

AND 49 OTHER WEIRD AND WONDERFUL SCIENTIFIC DISCOVERIES

Alice Harman

Sam Wedelich

 happy yak

Project Editor: Nancy Dickmann
Commissioning Editors: Catharine Robertson and Emily Pither
Project Designer: Claire Watson
Senior Designer: Mike Henson
Creative Director: Malena Stojić
Associate Publisher: Rhiannon Findlay
Senior Production Controller: Elizabeth Reardon

First published in 2025 by Happy Yak,
an imprint of The Quarto Group.
100 Cummings Center, Suite 265D.
Beverly, MA 01915, USA.
T (978) 282-9590 F (978) 283-2742
www.quarto.com

EEA Representation, WTS Tax d.o.o., Žanova ulica 3, 4000 Kranj, Slovenia

ISBN: 978 0 7112 9881 1
eISBN: 978 0 7112 9882 8

9 8 7 6 5 4 3 2 1

Manufactured in Guangzhou, China TT052025

MIX
Paper | Supporting
responsible forestry
FSC® C016973

DON'T try this at home! Please do not recreate any of the experiments or inventions in this book. Quarto Publishing plc cannot be held responsible for the experiments and inventions referred to in this book, or any recreations of them. All names and web addresses were correct at the time of printing.

FARTING FISH

AND **49** OTHER **WEIRD** AND **WONDERFUL** SCIENTIFIC DISCOVERIES

Alice Harman

Sam Wedelich

happy yak

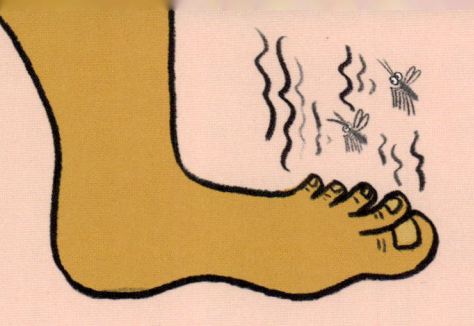

CONTENTS

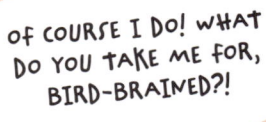

ANIMAL ANTICS

DO YOU KNOW MUCH ABOUT SCIENCE, PETE?

OF COURSE I DO! WHAT DO YOU TAKE ME FOR, BIRD-BRAINED?!

ODD BOD

SILLY	7/10
USEFUL	6/10
GROSS	1/10
SURPRISING	7/10

?!!

SCORING THE SCIENCE

The discoveries in this book can be silly, gross, useful, and surprising—sometimes all at the same time!

Look out for the score panel for each entry. All of them have won an Ig Nobel Prize, but we've given each discovery our own score in four different categories to see how they compare. See if you agree with them!

ALL IN GOOD TASTE

DO YOU MIND?

YIPPEE! MORE SAMPLES FOR MY LAB!

YOU'RE WELCOME!

INTRODUCTION

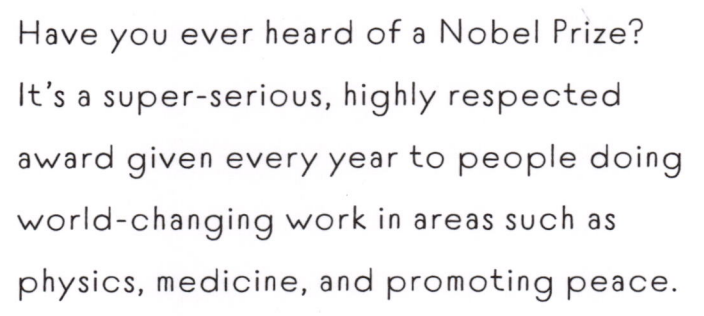

Have you ever heard of a Nobel Prize? It's a super-serious, highly respected award given every year to people doing world-changing work in areas such as physics, medicine, and promoting peace.

Now, have you ever heard of an Ig Nobel Prize? It's . . . a little different. This award celebrates some of the world's most surprising scientific work—from racing through a swimming pool full of syrup to using a remote-controlled helicopter to collect whale snot!

The Ig Nobel Prize ceremony is a hilariously chaotic night. Nobel Prize winners present awards made from flowerpots and mannequin heads and, if the speeches go on too long, an eight-year-old girl walks on stage and says "Please stop, I'm bored!"

Since the Ig Nobels began in 1991, ten prizes have been handed out each year. This book highlights 50 of the most fascinating prize-winning entries about animals, our bodies, food, and the brain. They each help us understand our world a bit better, even if they're telling us something we'd rather not know (like how many teens pick their nose AND eat it!).

THE GOAL OF THE IG NOBEL PRIZES IS TO MAKE YOU **LAUGH**, THEN MAKE YOU **THINK**!

WE SHOW THAT EVEN RESEARCH THAT SOUNDS BIZARRE CAN BE USEFUL AND INTERESTING.

Marc Abrahams, creator of the Ig Nobel Prize.

To find out more about the Ig Nobel Prizes, visit the official website at **www.improbable.com**

PAPER PLANE GAME

LOOK OUT FOR PAPER PLANES!

DON'T try this at home!

Making paper planes is a great way to get into the Ig Nobel spirit!

But don't try to recreate any of the experiments or inventions in this book—you could hurt yourself.

One much-loved (and suitably silly) tradition at the Ig Nobel Awards prize ceremony is to shower the stage and the award winners with paper planes.

People watching at home are encouraged to make videos of themselves throwing paper planes at the camera! The prize ceremony is for adults to watch, but these steps will show you how to make your own paper plane for fun.

HOW TO MAKE A PAPER PLANE

 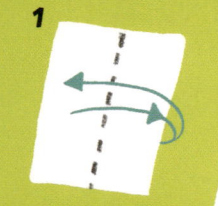      

Can you spot all the paper planes hidden in the rest of this book?

When you think you're done, turn to page 80 to check if you've found them all!

FINDING ANSWERS

The scientists who win Ig Nobel prizes might ask some odd questions, but they find the answers the same way all scientists do—by using the scientific method! In this process, you think of possible answers and then carry out experiments to see if you're right.

Have you noticed something strange that you'd love to investigate? You can use the scientific method too! This simple flow chart will guide you through the steps. Who knows, maybe you'll end up with your own Ig Nobel Prize . . . or even a Nobel Prize?!

1. QUESTION
What question do you want to find the answer to?

2. HYPOTHESIS
What do you predict the answer will be?

3. MATERIALS
What equipment do you need to help you investigate?

4. PROCEDURE
What steps will you take to try and answer your question? Think about how you can measure what you're trying to find out.

5. RESULTS
What happened in your investigation? Write down any measurements you collected.

6. CONCLUSION
What did you find out? Did you answer your question? Was your hypothesis correct?

Always check in with an adult before you start investigating, and let them know what you're doing. They can make sure it's safe, and supervise or help out if needed.

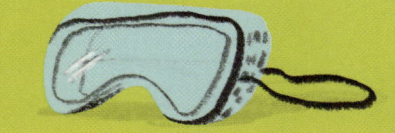

ANIMAL ANTICS

Our animal friends get up to some pretty weird things, so it's the job of scientists to investigate why they do what they do!

FARTING FISH

One dark night in the Scottish Highlands, underwater microphones picked up a mysterious noise. Then another. And another. Video cameras with **infra-red** lights captured streams of bubbles in the water. A breakthrough for hi-tech hunters of the Loch Ness Monster. . . ? Nope. It was scientists accidentally uncovering the secret language of fish farts.

These scientists were trying to find out if herrings can hear sounds made by predators such as whales and dolphins. Instead, they noticed the herrings making an unknown "high-pitched raspberry" sound as they released tiny gas bubbles from their butts! The scientists called these noises Fast Repetitive Tick Sounds (or, appropriately, FRTS for short). They only happened at night—and the more other herrings there were around, the more farting each fish did.

Underwater microphone

PFT PFT PFFFT PFFFT

PFFFT

PFFFFT PFFT PFT PFT

PFT PFT PFFFT

Herrings are smallish, silvery fish that swim around in huge groups called shoals or schools.

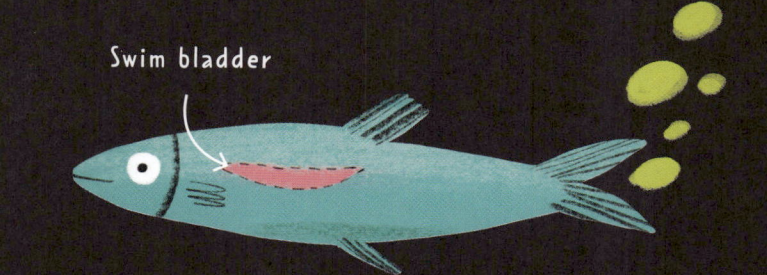

Swim bladder

The scientists discovered that the gas bubbles were made of air that the herrings had gulped from above the water's surface. This air was kept in their swim bladder—a special **organ** that helps many fish stay afloat.

It seems that some types of herring may deliberately fart to communicate with others in their shoal. Herrings have excellent hearing compared to other fish, and can hear high-pitched sounds. So at night, when herrings can't see each other, these farts could be their way of "talking" without alerting predators. However, now that humans know this secret, we could sneakily use herring FRTS to track shoals across the ocean.

Another team of scientists shared this Ig Nobel Prize because they also discovered herrings' farty chatter when the Swedish navy asked them to investigate some strange underwater sounds. The navy was worried it could be Russian submarines!

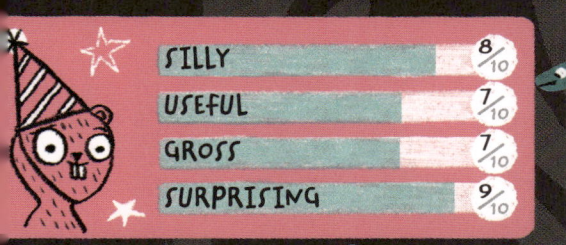

SILLY	8/10
USEFUL	7/10
GROSS	1/10
SURPRISING	9/10

11

EAR MITE EXPERIMENTS

DANCE PARTY!

DO THE EARWORM!

OH YEAH!

HEAR WE GO AGAIN!

WAIT FOR ME!

←

When vet Robert A. Lopez treated two cats with a bad ear mite infestation, he noticed that the family's young daughter complained of an itchy chest and stomach. She often cuddled the cats like dolls—and when the cats' infestation disappeared, so did her itching. Curious about whether cats' ear mites could infest humans, Dr. Lopez took some from a cat's ear and put them into his own left ear!

For the next month, he had bad pain and itching in this ear. Once the infestation cleared up, he repeated the self-experiment a second and third time! Each time, the infection was shorter and less severe, suggesting that it's possible to become **immune** to these mites. At the Ig Nobel awards, Dr. Lopez read out a poem he had written about ear mites!

Dr. Lopez said that he could hear and feel the mites moving around inside his ear. Yuck!

DO YOU THINK HE CAN HEAR US?

NOT SURE, LET'S TRY LOUDER!

SILLY		9/10
USEFUL		4/10
GROSS		10/10
SURPRISING		8/10

BEAR-PROOF ARMOR

How would you feel if you came face to face with a grizzly bear? Although they very rarely attack humans, grizzlies are huge and incredibly powerful, with razor-sharp claws and terrifying teeth . . .

Self-taught Canadian inventor Troy Hurtubise wanted to help people study grizzly bears up close without risking their lives. So he spent at least 15 years, and about $125,000 of his own money, trying to create an armored suit to allow humans to survive a bear attack.

The bear-proof suits were nearly 9 feet (2.7 meters) tall and mostly made of metal, plastic, and rubber. They were super-strong but very difficult to walk in!

As well as building the suit, Hurtubise also tested it himself in ridiculously dangerous ways. He had people hit and shoot him with weapons, run into him with trucks, and push him over huge drops. He also tried to encourage actual bear attacks, but they weren't interested in a fight. Experts think that the tall, strange-looking suit probably scared them off. You think?

SILLY	7/10
USEFUL	4/10
GROSS	1/10
SURPRISING	8/10

REINDEER REACTIONS

Svalbard reindeer lead a pretty relaxed, if chilly, life up near the North Pole. Most predators that typically hunt reindeer—such as wolves, lynxes, and brown bears—don't live in Svalbard. Polar bears do, but reports of attacks had always been rare.

However, something had changed. With more Arctic sea ice melting due to climate change, scientists suspected that polar bears and Svalbard reindeer were coming into contact more often.

One day, a research team saw a polar bear stalking a group of reindeer. At the time, the scientists had been measuring how these reindeer reacted to humans approaching them, dressed in dark hiking gear. But this gave them an idea . . .

The scientists decided to see how the reactions changed if they approached in a white polar bear disguise! The reindeer only let the "polar bear" get around half as close to them, before they got nervous and ran away.

The disguise was made from white clothes, with white tape and paper covering any gaps. A pulled-down white hat had cut-out eye holes and a drawn-on black nose.

COLLECTING WHALE SNOT

Out on the ocean's wind-whipped waves, a small boat bobs next to a gigantic whale. As the whale moves slowly away, a remote-controlled helicopter follows, hovering over its head. Suddenly, a fountain of snotty spray shoots up from the whale's blowhole, covering the helicopter—and the **petri dishes** it is carrying. Success!

Three scientists developed this ingenious snot-collection method after struggling to get close enough to large whales to take samples. Scientists can test whale snot for germs that cause serious diseases. This is really important because it's almost impossible to get a blood sample from a live whale in the wild.

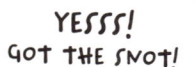

YESSS! GOT THE SNOT!

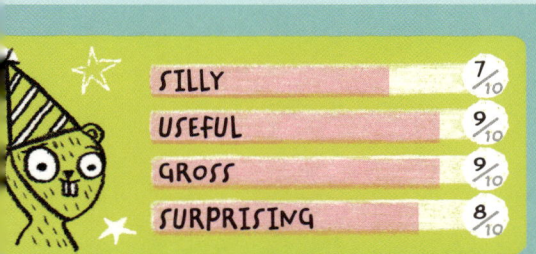

SILLY	7/10
USEFUL	9/10
GROSS	9/10
SURPRISING	8/10

Experts think that humans may be accidentally infecting whales with deadly germs, by polluting the ocean and touching whales while on boat trips. The more we know about whales' health, the better we can try to protect them.

A whale's blowhole is like its nostril. It breathes out air full of snot and **water vapor**.

DOG VS CAT FLEAS

The flea is one of nature's greatest jumpers. This special power means that it can launch itself on to an animal host, to feed on its blood. Humans often come across two flea species: dog fleas (*Ctenocephalides canis*) and cat fleas (*Ctenocephalides felis*). But which would win in a high-jump or long-jump competition?! Three scientists in France decided to find out.

DOG FLEA   CAT FLEA

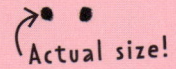

Actual size!

CHEAT!

LONG-JUMP RESULTS

Dog fleas   12 in (30.4 cm)
Cat fleas   7.8 in (19.9 cm)

SHOW OFF!.

HIGH-JUMP RESULTS

Dog fleas   6.1 in (15.5 cm)
Cat fleas   5.2 in (13.2 cm)

AND THE WINNER IS . . . DOG FLEAS!

WHATEVER.

Gold medals for the dog fleas! The cat fleas can still jump around 50 times their own body length, though. That's like an adult human jumping over six buses in a row!

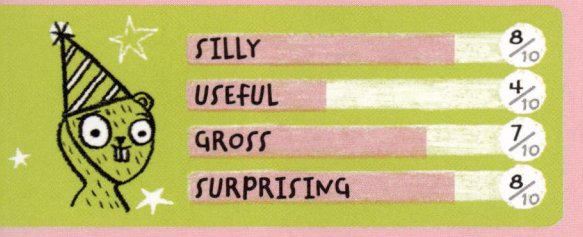

SILLY	8/10
USEFUL	4/10
GROSS	7/10
SURPRISING	8/10

Fleas power their lightning-quick leaps by squeezing parts of their body together like a coiled spring. When they release this stored energy, it propels them through the air.

WHEEEE!

CANINE TRANSLATOR

If you have a pet dog, have you ever wondered what they are thinking? Maybe you need BowLingual, an electronic device that can supposedly translate a dog's barks into human words! It was created by the Takara toy company in Japan, with the help of an expert in voice **analysis** and the head of a veterinary hospital.

To use the BowLingual, you attach a small microphone to a dog's collar. When the dog barks, growls, whines, and so on, the device "reads" these noises and matches them to a set of sound-wave patterns. It can apparently work out if a dog is happy, sad, scared, frustrated, wants something, or is just feeling talkative!

The dog's mood is translated into one of 200 phrases, which show up—along with pictures—on the screen of a hand-held device.

WOOOF!

woof woof?

woof woof woof . . . ?

SILLY		7/10
USEFUL		6/10
GROSS		1/10
SURPRISING		7/10

There are mixed reviews of the BowLingual's accuracy, but it has sold in its hundreds of thousands. There is also a Meowlingual for cats!

DOG MOOD TRANSLATOR

I LOVE YOU!

CAN WE GO TO THE PARK?

ALSO, TREATS

OVERALL MOOD:

DUNG BEETLES
AND THE MILKY WAY

The Milky Way is our **galaxy**. On clear, dark nights, we can see part of it arcing like a glowing river of starlight through the sky. Scientists have found that, for dung beetles, this magical sight is also an excellent guide for rolling a big chunk of poop in the right direction.

Dung beetles collect poop to eat, then roll it away as fast as possible to stop others stealing it. They must travel in a straight line to avoid accidentally circling back to the would-be thieves. Scientists from Sweden and South Africa noticed that the beetles could still **navigate** successfully on dark, moonless nights, and decided to set up an experiment.

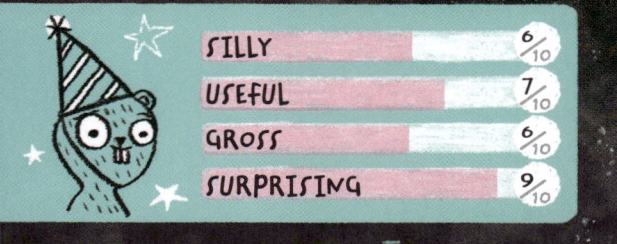

SILLY 6/10
USEFUL 7/10
GROSS 6/10
SURPRISING 9/10

The scientists placed some dung beetles in a circle-shaped arena, measuring 6.6 feet (2 metres) across, on a table outside. The arena had high sides to block out nearby landmarks that the beetles might use to navigate.

THE TRIALS OF THE DUNG BEETLE

On cloudy nights, the dung beetles struggled to roll dung balls in straight lines from the center to the edge of the arena.

OK, DAVE? HERE WE ARE AGAIN, ROLLING POOP.

But on particularly clear, dark nights, they did this much more quickly than normal.

WOW, DAVE, YOU'RE QUICK TONIGHT!

Dung beetles have weak eyesight, so scientists suspected they were using the Milky Way rather than individual stars.

HEY! YOU CALLING ME WEAK?

The scientists moved the experiment setup into the Johannesburg Planetarium, under a video projection of the night sky. They could turn the stars and Milky Way on and off.

When they turned off the stars, the beetles could still travel in pretty straight lines.

However, when they turned off the Milky Way but left on some stars, the beetles found it harder to do.

Back out under the night sky, the scientists put tiny hats on the beetles to block their view of the Milky Way and stars—and they wandered around in aimless circles.

I'VE TOTALLY GOT THIS.

NOPE, HAVEN'T GOT IT!

OH NO, NOT THESE STUPID HATS AGAIN!

GLORIOUS PLAY OF LIGHT ON THE WATER!

DO YOU THINK THEY'VE GOT A PICNIC TO SHARE?

SUCH BOLD BRUSHWORK!

BUT ARE WE ABSOLUTELY SURE IT'S THE RIGHT WAY UP?

SILLY	8/10
USEFUL	4/10
GROSS	2/10
SURPRISING	9/10

ARTY PIGEONS

Can you tell a Picasso painting from a Monet masterpiece? Well, apparently pigeons can! Scientists in Japan successfully trained two groups of pigeons to peck on a certain spot only when they were shown artworks by either Pablo Picasso or Claude Monet.

The scientists then tested the pigeons with different artworks to the ones used for training, and found that the birds could recognize each artist's style around 90% of the time.

Pablo Picasso's Cubist art usually includes strong colors and sharp, bold lines. Monet's Impressionist art typically uses softer colors and blurry shapes. However, scientists also showed the birds the artworks in black-and-white, out of focus and upside-down, and they still mostly chose correctly!

The pigeons could also spot the style of Impressionist or Cubist works from other artists, such as Cézanne and Braque.

CAT-PROOF KEYBOARDS

FNNNRYHGUHFFLPPPYRRRRRRR. That's what can happen when your pet cat decides to march right across your computer keyboard. And if the cat stomps on the right shortcut keys, it could end up deleting important files, uninstalling software, and crashing the computer!

When this exact thing happened to computer scientist Chris Niswander's sister (thanks to her cat, Amos), it inspired him to create the PawSense computer program.

Niswander observed cats' movements and experimented by walking cardboard-cutout paws over a keyboard. Then he wrote code to recognise "cat-like typing"—typically heavy, oddly timed pressing of random key combinations.

When PawSense detects a cat, it locks the keyboard until someone clicks a certain button or types "human." If your cat is genius enough to do that, you might want to let it stay on there to write your homework for you!

ERROR!

ARRRGGHHHH TIBBLES, NOT AGAIN!

SILLY	8/10
USEFUL	7/10
GROSS	4/10
SURPRISING	6/10

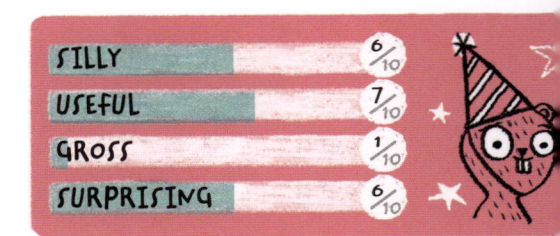
DUCKLINGS SWIM IN A LINE

When most people see a line of fluffy ducklings swimming behind their mother, they just think "Aw, sweet!" But this team of scientists thought, "Why?" They studied families of ducks and other water birds, and used math to work out how staying in a neat single file helped ducklings save their energy.

When a duckling swims, it creates waves in the water. At the same time, the waves push back against the duckling—this **force** is called "wave drag." The scientists found that when a duckling swims at a certain distance behind its mother, it can ride the wave her body creates.

This can hugely reduce the duckling's wave drag, making it easier for it to swim. It can even—at a particular "sweet spot" distance—actually push the duckling forward. Each duckling in the line passes along waves to the ones behind, so they all get an easy ride as long as they stick close together.

A bird's-eye view of the wave drag effect on the line of ducklings.

MOOOM, DILLON LOOKED AT ME FUNNY!

UGH, STOP PUSHING ME!

ARE WE NEARLY THERE YET?

22

WOMBAT POOP CUBES

Bare-nosed wombats are cuddly-looking Australian **marsupials** with a strange natural gift: they're the only animal known to poop cubes. Some scientists think this is because wombats like to mark their **territory** by pooping on rocks and logs, and—unlike rounded shapes—cubes don't roll away.

Wombats don't have square butts, so how do they make these cubes? A team of scientists found out by studying the **intestines** of wombats that had sadly been killed by cars. Some lower parts of a wombat's intestine are stretchy and some are stiff, and they squeeze at different speeds to shape poop into cubes.

By the time wombat poop reaches this part of the intestine, it is very dry, since almost all the water and nutrients have been absorbed. This helps create the cubes' sharp edges and corners.

Researchers think that these findings could inspire new ways to shape and create products, and even help detect colon cancer in humans.

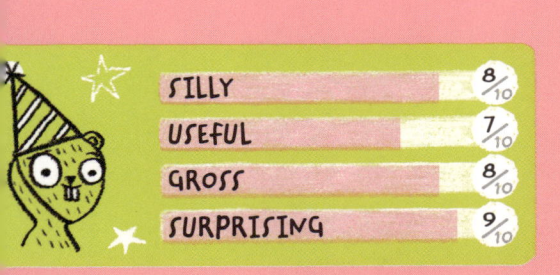

SILLY	8/10
USEFUL	7/10
GROSS	8/10
SURPRISING	9/10

LEVITATING FROGS

When people think of "levitation," they likely imagine a magician's trick that lifts a person up and holds them floating in mid-air. What they probably don't have in mind is a confused frog, spinning around 6.5 feet (2 metres) off the ground inside an extremely powerful magnet . . .

This impossible-seeming levitation is possible because frogs, like most living things, are diamagnetic. That means that a frog is usually non-magnetic, but when placed near a magnet its **molecules** create their own magnetic field. This field pushes back against the magnet's field.

If you place a frog inside a strong enough magnetic field, the force of the frog's molecules pushing up away from the magnet is stronger than the gravity pulling them down to Earth. This means that the frog stays floating in the air, just as scientist Andre Geim showed in a laboratory's super-strong **electromagnet** machine.

ERRR . . . WEIRD!

HOW DOES IT FEEL TO BE THE WORLD'S FIRST LEVITATING FROG?

Geim and his team decided to try levitating . . .

strawberries, hazelnuts, cherry tomatoes, fish, a grasshopper, a mouse, and a frog.

They had to use a super-strong magnet, around 1,000 times stronger than a fridge magnet. Each experiment was a success, and the levitation didn't harm the animals (or plants).

LOOK, MA! NO HANDS . . . OR FEET!

Although it hasn't been tried yet, it should be possible to levitate a person! You would just need an extremely strong magnet, and a big enough machine to fit them inside. Would you want to try it?

SILLY	$7/10$
USEFUL	$9/10$
GROSS	$3/10$
SURPRISING	$9/10$

This levitation science has other exciting potential uses too. They include controlling **satellites** traveling around planets, building cheaper super-high-speed trains, and creating near-weightless conditions for experiments on Earth instead of launching them into space.

Ten years after his Ig Nobel Prize, Andre Geim won the Nobel Prize for Physics (for different research)! He is the first person to ever win both individual prizes.

WHEEEEEEEEEEEEE!

QUIZ TIME!

1. Why do ducklings stay in a neat line behind their mother?

2. What shape is wombat poop?

3. How did the inventor of the PawSense computer program train it to recognize cat paw prints?

4. Name three living things that scientist Andre Geim levitated with an electromagnet.

5. Can you name one of the artists whose paintings pigeons were able to identify in an experiment?

6. Do reindeer run away faster from scientists in dark hiking gear or a white polar-bear disguise?

7. What type of fish did scientists overhear farting, apparently to talk to each other?

8. Why on Earth would a scientist want to collect whale snot?

9. How did scientists block dung beetles' view of the Milky Way in their experiment?

10. Which can jump higher—a cat flea or a dog flea?

NOW CHECK YOUR ANSWERS ON PAGE 80.

HOW DID YOU DO?

ODD BOD

Our bodies are amazing—and sometimes also pretty gross. Luckily, science is on hand to explain the mysteries of how our bodies work.

REAL STINK

FAKE STINK

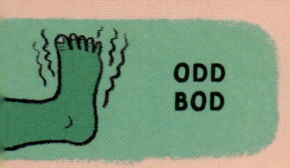

CHEESY FEET AND MOSQUITOES

Do you ever peel off your socks after a long day and get a serious whiff of stinky cheese?! Foot odor is a natural, if smelly, part of being a human, but in some parts of the world it can be deadly.

Certain female mosquitoes seem to be attracted to human foot odor. They also often carry a **parasite** that causes malaria, a serious disease that they can pass on through their bites.

Two scientists wanted to find out if mosquitoes would be attracted to Limburger cheese, known for smelling like stinky feet. They set up an experiment with two traps, one of which smelled like Limburger cheese. The mosquitoes preferred the cheesy trap!

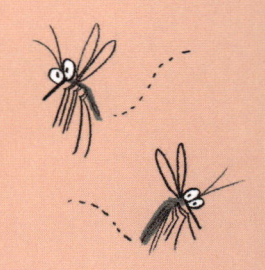

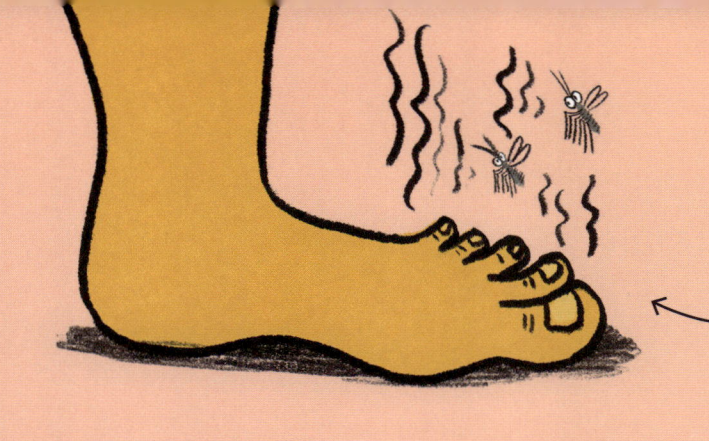

Limburger cheese ripens in a moist environment at around 90–93°F (32–34°C). This is similar to the warm, sweaty micro-habitat found between our toes. Mmmmm.

The experiment's result makes more sense than it might seem. Limburger cheese is made using **bacteria** that are closely related to the bacteria often found living between human toes.

These bacteria produce similar **fatty acids**, according to analysis of human toe scrapings (*eeewwww*) and Limburger cheese odor. Different mosquitoes seem to be attracted to the smell of certain fatty acids on human skin.

So, although this cheesy-feet science might seem silly, it could actually save lives. Scientists have now **extracted** fatty acids from Limburger cheese—and other substances—to help develop baited traps that mosquitoes find irresistible. The hope is that these traps will attract and kill malaria-carrying mosquitoes before they can infect humans.

SILLY	7/10
USEFUL	9/10
GROSS	9/10
SURPRISING	9/10

OOOH—WHAT'S THAT DELIGHTFUL FRAGRANCE?!

LIMBURGER CHEESE-CAKE

STINKY GOODNESS!

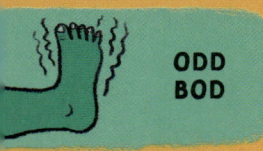

STINKY FEET AWARENESS

Do you think your feet are stinky? Whatever you think, you're probably right! A team of scientists in Japan discovered that people who think they have foot odor, do—and people who think they don't, don't. This isn't as obvious as it might seem, since the way we see—or smell—ourselves can be very different to how others do.

This foot odor **study** also involved scientists trying to find the exact chemicals that make feet smelly. An unlucky panel of sniffers compared the smell of different **artificial** foot-odor-like creations, and the scientists studied which chemicals they shared with genuine "sock extracts."

Scientists discovered several fatty acids on smelly feet, especially one called iso-valeric acid that wasn't found on non-smelly feet at all. This knowledge could help develop better foot-odor-fighting substances—hooray!

PLEASE, I JUST NEED YOUR SWEATY SOCKS!

IT'S FOR SCIENCE!

Scientists first got ten people to exercise for half an hour. Then they put their sweaty socks inside a lab **apparatus** for five hours to isolate the smelly substances.

SILLY	8/10
USEFUL	6/10
GROSS	10/10
SURPRISING	3/10

PEE-YEW!!!

REAL STINK

FAKE STINK

EW, WHO DID THAT STINKY FART?

NOT ME, PHEW!

ODD BOD

AIRTIGHT FABRIC

STINK-PROOF FILTER

TICKETS

The scientific term for fart gas is "flatus."

FART-PROOF UNDERPANTS

Everybody farts! It's a totally natural, and sometimes pretty funny, part of life. But there are times when you'd rather not let rip a real rotten-eggy stinker! And some people actually have medical conditions that can make them do lots of uncontrollable, extra-smelly farts.

Psychologist Buck Weimer's wife, Arlene, was one of these people, so he spent years researching how to help her. He found that activated charcoal was known to reduce strong smells by absorbing the chemicals that cause them.

So he invented *Underease Underwear*, which are airtight underpants that force farts to escape through a removable charcoal **filter**. This thin layer safely traps the smelly chemicals while allowing the rest of the gas through.

Underease Underwear is no longer in business, but the fart-proof technology lives on! Other companies still sell fart-proof underpants with charcoal filters. This often helps people with certain illnesses feel more comfortable to travel and spend time in groups.

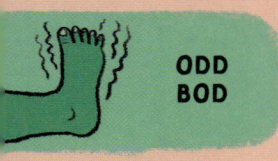

ANTI-GAS GIANT

Alan Kligerman's fart-fighting inventions—including LACTAID® and beano®—have made him a multi-millionaire!

LACTAID® is made for lactose-intolerant people, who often get lots of farty gas, a stomachache, and diarrhea if they eat or drink milk products. It's pretty common to be lactose-intolerant, as Kligerman discovered when he delivered milk as a young man. Some people couldn't buy milk because it made them fart too much!

After studying dairy science at university, Kligerman experimented with using an enzyme to break down the lactose in milk, so lactose-intolerant people could enjoy it too.

He eventually created LACTAID®, a **supplement** containing an enzyme called lactase (with an "a"), to take alongside dairy foods. It's still a big seller today!

Enzymes are natural substances —usually **proteins**—in our bodies. They speed up chemical reactions.

INTRODUCING...

Many foods and drinks can cause a build-up of digestive gas, which can result in lots of farts! They often contain **carbohydrates** that the human small intestine can find difficult to absorb or digest. When these undigested carbohydrates move into the large intestine, and "friendly" bacteria break them down there, it can create farty gas.

If we have enough of certain enzymes in our small intestine, it can help break down foods before they travel into the large intestine. Kligerman used this knowledge to invent beano®, a supplement that contains one of these enzymes—alpha-galactosidase. It helps the body break down food molecules in the small intestine, preventing gas and therefore farts!

Fart-producing foods can vary from person to person, but common culprits include beans, peanuts, cabbage, onions, and broccoli.

33

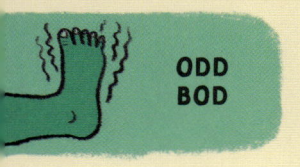

SILLY	9/10
USEFUL	2/10
GROSS	3/10
SURPRISING	8/10

OLD MEN'S BIG EARS

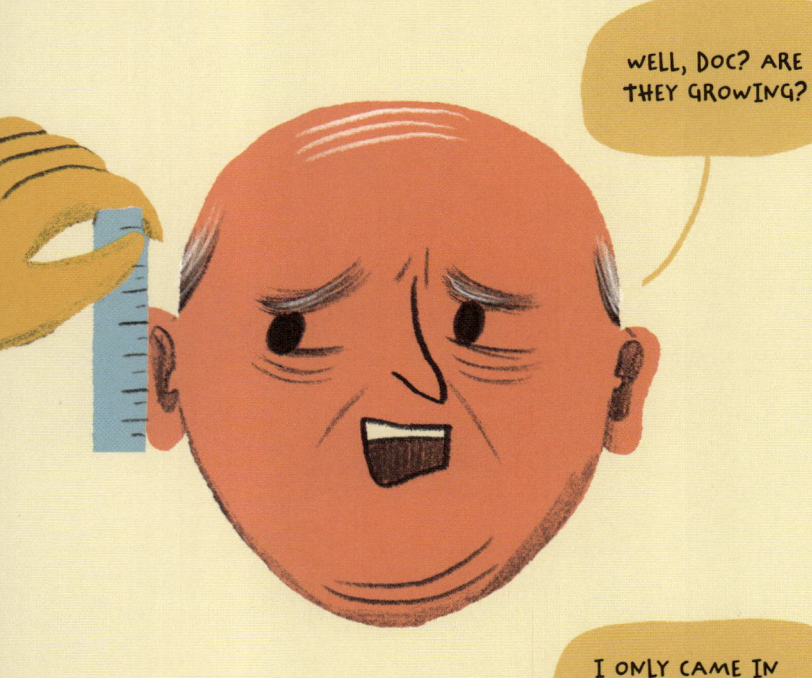

WELL, DOC? ARE THEY GROWING?

Have you ever noticed that old men have particularly big ears? One group of family physicians decided to find out if it was true that men's ears keep growing throughout their entire lives. They used their own patients as subjects—with their permission, of course!

The physicians measured the left ears of 206 randomly selected men and women, ranging from 30 to over 90 years old. Using a see-through ruler, the doctors noted the length (in millimeters) of each person's ear, from the top to the lowest point. After **analyzing** these measurements, they found that as adults —not just men!—get older, their ears get 0.22 mm bigger (on average) each year.

I ONLY CAME IN FOR MY FLU SHOT!

Later studies in Italy and Japan also appear to show that people's ears get bigger throughout their life. So, is it true that our ears never stop growing? Well, maybe ... or it could just be that ears sag and lengthen with age, as our skin gets less elastic and gravity pulls it down.

Over 50 years, adults' ears get about 0.5 inch (1 cm) bigger— a noticeable difference!

1 in
2 in
3 in
4 in

TEENAGE NOSE PICKING

Do teenagers pick their noses? According to the respected psychiatrists Dr. Chittaranjan Andrade and Dr. BS Srihari, who studied 200 teens, the answer is a big, boogerlicious yes!

Almost all of the teenagers who filled in the scientists' survey revealed that they picked their nose. (If there had been a hidden-camera study on the others, how many do you think would have been caught out with a finger up their nostril?!)

Around half of the self-confessed nose-pickers enjoyed a booger-mining session four or more times a day. A committed few (over 7%) said they picked their nose 20 or more times daily! Only a small number (4.5%) admitted to eating their boogers after picking them. But around a quarter of all the teens said they sometimes had nose bleeds from picking their nose. Ouch!

At the Ig Nobel prize ceremony, Dr. Andrade apparently explained: "Some people poke their nose into other people's business. I made it my business to poke my business into other people's noses."

SO, LIKE, WHAT SHOULD WE PLAY NEXT?!

EWWW!

SILLY	9/10
USEFUL	2/10
GROSS	9/10
SURPRISING	2/10

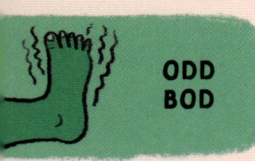

GREEN HAIR MYSTERY

In the small Swedish town of Anderslöv, some people suddenly began to notice that their usually-blonde hair was turning green! They were very confused, and understandably nervous that whatever was doing this might be causing more serious harm.

An environmental engineer named Johan Pettersson was brought in to investigate. He tested the town's water supply, but found nothing unusual at all. So he tested the water coming out of the faucets in the green-haired people's houses. Aha! This water had up to four times the normal amount of copper in it.

It turned out that all the people with green hair lived in new houses, with copper pipes that apparently hadn't been well coated enough. So when water sat in the pipes overnight, and was then heated for people's showers, it absorbed so much copper that it turned their hair green!

HEY, WHAT'S WITH THE GREEN HAIR?

HEY!! I'M TRYING TO SHOWER HERE!

Copper turns green over time when it reacts with oxygen. New York's famously green Statue of Liberty is made of copper and was originally reddish-brown!

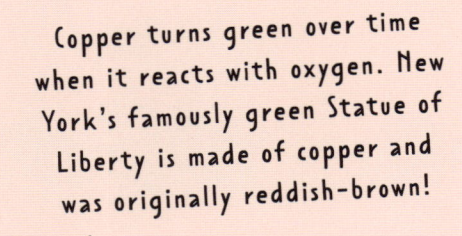

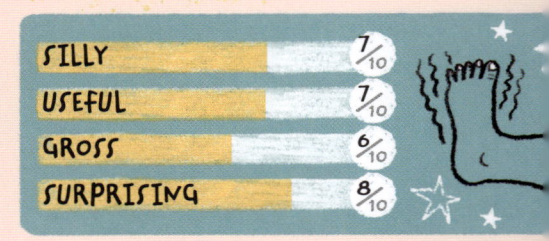

SILLY	7/10
USEFUL	7/10
GROSS	6/10
SURPRISING	8/10

BRRRR!

SILLY		8/10
USEFUL		2/10
GROSS		7/10
SURPRISING		1/10

WET UNDERWEAR

It probably feels like common sense that wearing wet underwear in the cold would make you feel cold and uncomfortable, right? But science can be surprising, so it's always worth properly testing out what might seem obvious.

The eight people taking part in this experiment wore either wet or dry long underwear, and sat in a cold test chamber for an hour. They had their temperature taken throughout the experiment. They also filled in forms every ten minutes, answering questions about how wet or dry their underwear felt, how much they were sweating and/or shivering, and how comfortable they felt.

The unsurprising—but now scientifically proven—results were that sitting around in wet underwear makes you feel wet, cold, and uncomfortable. An astonishing discovery! (That anyone who's ever done gym class on a cold, rainy day in winter could have told you.)

The long underwear came in a variety of thicknesses and fabrics—including wool, cotton, and plastic. The thicker underwear felt more comfortable, while the material seemed to make little difference.

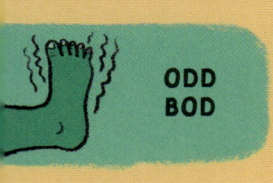

SILLY		8/10
USEFUL		7/10
GROSS		8/10
SURPRISING		7/10

The diaper-changing machine is designed to store up to ten diaper nappies, without smells escaping.

DIAPER-CHANGING MACHINE

Did you know that a new baby can need their diaper changed more than ten times a day?! Luckily, engineer Dr. Iman Farahbakhsh has helped out tired (and often poop-covered) parents and carers by inventing an automatic machine to change diapers and wash backsides!

The machine is still in development, but its design has been patented (protected by law from being used or copied without permission). It uses robot parts to automatically perform all the steps involved in baby-changing: removing the dirty diaper, washing the baby's backside, drying it with warm air, then putting on a fresh diaper. All at the press of a button!

The whole process should take around two minutes, on average, and the machine has been designed to play music and cartoons to keep the baby calm and entertained. Do you think you'd like being inside a machine that automatically washes and dries your butt?!

GENIUS TOILET

Nowadays, we can use **smart** technology to track and analyze everything from how well we sleep to whether we're getting enough exercise. But what about our pees and poops? It may sound funny, but they can actually tell us a lot about our health.

The idea for a "smart toilet," which can analyze urine (pee) and stool (poop) samples, has been around since the 1970s. But the Stanford Toilet is one of the most impressive recent examples. It has all sorts of testing gadgets, including pee-testing strips and a computer system to check poop against the Bristol Stool Form Scale's seven types (ranging from dry, hard lumps to entirely liquid).

The Stanford Toilet also analyzes when, and for how long, someone is using it— and a camera can even tell who they are. Apparently every butt is unique, just like a fingerprint!

CONGRATS!

YOUR POOP IS:

The Stanford Toilet's tests could help detect everything from infections to certain types of cancer. During the Covid-19 pandemic, scientists even looked into using smart toilets for Covid testing!

SILLY	5/10
USEFUL	9/10
GROSS	8/10
SURPRISING	7/10

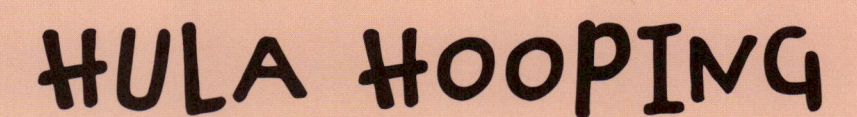

HULA HOOPING

Can you keep a hula hoop spinning around your middle? It's not as simple as it looks! Two respected scientists analyzed the various movements and forces at work during hula hooping, and found that it's actually a pretty complicated balancing act.

To keep the hula hoop from falling to the ground, you need to apply force in two directions at once: horizontally to keep it circling, and upward to keep it from falling. Most people use their hips and ankles for the circular motion and their knees for the upward force.

Even when the hoop is spinning smoothly round, it is an unstable balance. The scientists found that when hula hoopers were distracted, their hip-ankle system and knee system easily fell out of rhythm. Sometimes they could rebalance the hoop by moving a little faster, but sometimes it fell to the floor.

WHEEEE HULA HULA!

BARK! BARK!

FIDO, YOU PUT ME OFF!

Today, an Australian woman named Marawa Ibrahim holds the world record for hula hooping-she can spin 200 plastic hoops at once!

MORE BLUE FLUFF??! WHERE DID YOU COME FROM?

SILLY		9/10
USEFUL		1/10
GROSS		8/10
SURPRISING		7/10

BELLY BUTTON FLUFF

One day, a man called in to a science show on Australian radio to ask its host, Dr. Karl, two very important questions: Why do I get belly button fluff? And why is it blue?!

Dr. Karl didn't know the answers and couldn't find any scientific studies on this subject. So, the radio show team decided to set up their own online survey! After two months, they had almost 4,800 responses.

The responses showed that only two out of three people had any belly button fluff. They were more likely to have it if they were older, hairy, and male, with an innie (rather than an outie) belly button.

One theory is that hair on the belly catches fluff from clothes and carries it up into the belly button. However, some people with little or no belly hair still had fluff.

Blue is a common color for clothing, so that could explain the caller's blue belly button fluff. But, mysteriously, two out of three people said the color of theirs didn't match their clothes at all!

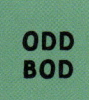 **ODD BOD**

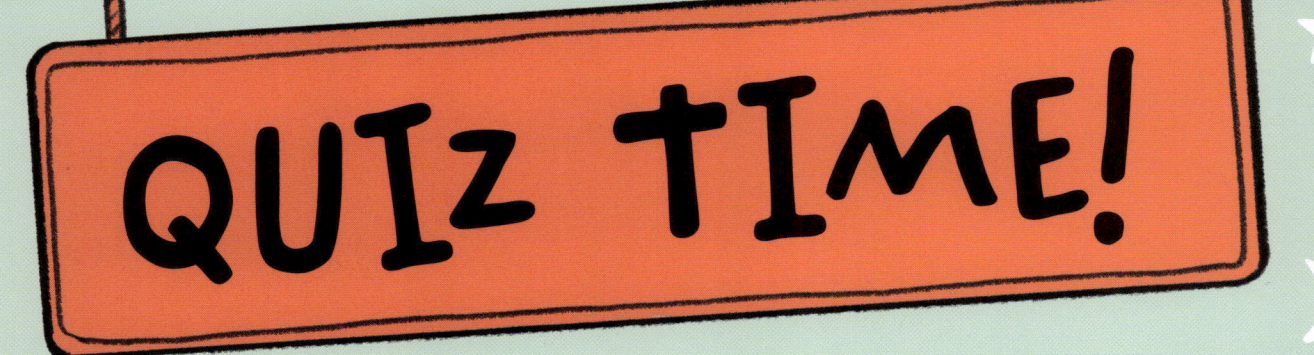

QUIz TIME!

1. How do you keep a hula hoop from falling to the ground?

2. Do people's ears get bigger throughout their life?

3. Which cheese smells particularly like stinky feet?

4. Name one of the Stanford Toilet's smart gadgets.

5. What percentage of teenagers in a study admitted to eating their boogers?

6. What is an enzyme that can break down the lactose in milk? (Clue: It's only one letter different!)

7. What do scientists think iso-valeric acid might cause?

8. If someone has to sit around in wet long underwear, would they be more or less comfortable if that underwear was thicker?

9. What metal was responsible for turning people's hair green in Anderslöv, Sweden?

10. What is the anti-smell filter in *Underease Underwear* fart-proof underpants made of?

NOW CHECK YOUR ANSWERS ON PAGE 80. HOW DID YOU DO?

ALL IN GOOD TASTE

Why do scientists spend so much time studying food? Because everybody needs to eat, of course!

COOKIE DUNKING

Do you like to dunk cookies, maybe into a glass of milk or a mug of hot chocolate? If so, have you ever watched your dunked cookie suddenly break apart, collapsing into a sad, soggy sludge at the bottom of your drink? The worst!

Luckily, Dr. Len Fisher has studied the physics of cookie dunking, and shared his scientifically proven method. Instead of holding the top of the cookie and dipping it in vertically, the trick is to pinch the cookie's outside edge and dunk it almost horizontally, like you're placing it on the surface of your drink.

With either type of dunk, the drink needs to be cool enough not to hurt fingertips. A cookie dunked in the usual, vertical way only lasts about 3.5 to 5 seconds, depending on the type of cookie. But one that's been "scientifically dunked" lasts a whopping 14 to 20 seconds before collapsing. A clear winner!

For an even longer dunk, Fisher recommended using a cookie coated on one side with chocolate—and keeping the chocolatey side facing up.

I THINK THIS WAY OF DUNKING IS SUPERIOR - AND I CAN PROVE IT!

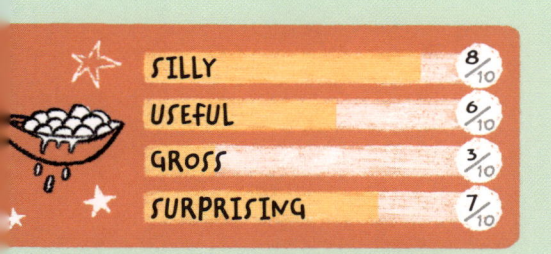

SILLY		8/10
USEFUL		6/10
GROSS		3/10
SURPRISING		7/10

Studies have shown that dunking can make a cookie taste nicer! A longer dunk seems to give a bigger flavor boost, but the combination of cookie and drink also makes a difference.

So, what's the science behind the "scientific dunk?" Firstly, a cookie is basically made up of tiny starch grains, glued together by sugar. When you dunk a cookie, liquid is sucked into the tiny holes and tunnels between its crumbs.

The liquid makes the starch grains swell up and soften, causing the wet part of the cookie to weaken and break apart. Hot liquids also dissolve the cookie's sugar "glue" so it breaks apart more quickly.

To avoid a dunked cookie collapsing into mush, part of it needs to stay dry. In a typical dunk, the liquid soaks the cookie all the way through sooner than in a scientific dunk.

This is because, in a typical dunk, the liquid is on both sides of the cookie and so only has to travel halfway through the cookie to wet it completely. In a scientific dunk, the liquid has to travel the entire thickness of the cookie—that is, twice as far—to do this.

Cookie
Hot drink

TYPICAL DUNK

Cookie
Hot drink

SCIENTIFIC DUNK

VERY VITAL RESEARCH . . . A PUBLIC SERVICE, REALLY . . . BUT, ANYTHING FOR SCIENCE!

YUMMY-SOUNDING FOOD

Imagine biting into two **identical** apples, one after the other. The first apple makes a satisfying crunch, but the second makes a soft, squelching noise. Which one do you think you would enjoy more?

Our sense of taste doesn't work alone—how things smell has a big effect on it, as does how they look. And according to a 2005 study, how food sounds can also alter how it tastes!

Two scientists asked volunteers to eat potato chips while wearing headphones and sitting in front of a microphone. The microphones picked up the chip-crunching sounds before they came through the volunteers' headphones. Sometimes they were electronically changed to be louder at a higher pitch.

The volunteers were asked to push on foot pedals to vote on how crispy and fresh each potato chip seemed. The scientists discovered that when the sound of the crunch was made louder at a higher pitch, people thought the potato chips tasted crisper and fresher.

The volunteers had to bite into each potato chip just once, with their front teeth. This helped keep the chip-crunching experience as similar as possible each time.

SILLY		8/10
USEFUL		5/10
GROSS		4/10
SURPRISING		7/10

CRUNCH! CRUNCH!

WAIT! I'LL TAKE A SAMPLE OF THAT!

UGH! GROSS!

ALL IN GOOD TASTE

CHEWING-GUM BACTERIA

City streets around the world often have one gross thing in common . . . globs of spat-out gum stuck all over the sidewalks. Ew!

A team of scientists in Spain wondered if the bacteria found on this gum was the same everywhere. They studied lumps of discarded, chewed gum from Spain, France, Singapore, Greece, and Türkiye, scraping up slivers of each piece at regular times over twelve weeks.

Whatever the location, just after the gum was spat out it was mostly covered in similar types of oral (mouth) bacteria. But over a few weeks, bacteria from the gum's new surroundings largely took over, and these were often very different from place to place.

EVIDENCE 2.17 (UNDER TABLE!)

Some oral bacteria remained trapped in the sticky gum for a surprisingly long time. This knowledge could potentially be used to help solve crimes!

LUWAK POOP COFFEE

SILLY	6/10
USEFUL	2/10
GROSS	9/10
SURPRISING	9/10

When you imagine the world's most expensive coffee, usually costing over $60 a cup, you might picture it covered with gold leaf or perhaps sprinkled with powdered diamond. But it's actually poop that makes it so pricey!

Kopi luwak is made from coffee berries that have been eaten and pooped out by an animal called a luwak, or palm civet. It is a rare delicacy in Indonesia, and was little-known outside the country until people such as John Martinez (who won this Ig Nobel Prize for his efforts) started selling it in the USA and beyond.

Fans say that the coffee is unique and particularly smooth, partly because the luwak only eats the ripest, best-quality berries. Other coffee experts say it tastes terrible, and it's only the funny story that people are paying for.

Once the civet has pooped out the coffee beans, they are cleaned (thank goodness!), then dried out and roasted.

HURRAH, I'VE FOUND A POOP!

LUWAK COFFEE

Since kopi luwak has become so popular, it's led to wild luwaks being captured and kept in cruel conditions in small cages. Animal rights groups have now convinced many stores and cafés to stop selling it—good work!

COWS WITH NAMES

If you were a dairy farmer, what would you name your cows? You could go for classics like Bessie and Buttercup, or maybe a particularly lively one could be Milkshake! Whatever you choose, the fact that you've named them at all apparently means that they'll produce more milk.

Scientists asked more than 500 dairy farmers in the UK about how they managed their herds, including whether or not they named all their cows. Almost half of them did name them, and these cows gave over 55 gallons (250 liters, or about 1,000 glasses) more milk each year!

This is likely because individually naming cows suggests a more caring approach, in which each cow gets a bit more one-to-one attention. This personal touch can make cows feel happier and more relaxed. Many scientific studies have shown that cows' feelings toward the humans who care for them affects how much milk they produce.

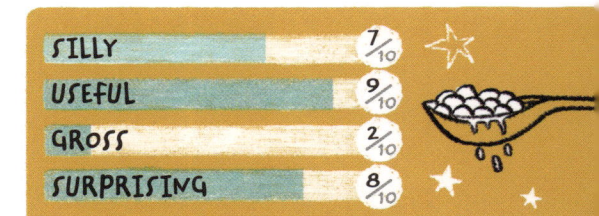

SILLY	7/10
USEFUL	9/10
GROSS	2/10
SURPRISING	8/10

YOU'RE MY BEST FRIENDS!

MIKE

DAISY

MABEL

LICKING ROCKS

What would you think if you saw someone pick up a rock from the side of the road and lick it? Your first thought might not be "Ah, a scientist at work!" But there are a few reasons why scientists—particularly geologists and paleontologists—can find it helpful to lick rocks.

Jan Zalasiewicz, a geologist and paleontologist, won his Ig Nobel prize for explaining how licking rocks can make it easier to spot any **fossils** (remains of living things) and **minerals** (such as metals and gems) that they contain. He also talked about how scientists, especially in the past, have used their sense of taste to describe and identify different types of rocks.

Geologists study the solid Earth itself, while paleontologists study the history of life on Earth. Both often spend a lot of time looking at rocks!

MMMM, SALTY!

LICKED

TO BE LICKED

READER ALERT!

Don't lick any rocks
(unless a trained geologist
has told you it's safe)!

ALL IN GOOD TASTE

Rocks are made up of one or more minerals, and some of these have distinctive tastes. The mineral halite tastes salty—in fact, it's used to make table salt! So, scientists can lick rocks to see if they contain halite. If a rock tastes salty and bitter, this could mean it contains another mineral called sylvite. Urgh, sylvite doesn't exactly sound yummy, does it?

A human tongue is very sensitive to texture as well as taste, which can be very helpful to scientists. They can lick or chew a pinch of sediment (powdered rock) to tell how big the grains in it are. Sand particles feel quite hard and sharp, while clay particles feel more like mud. And if scientists lick part of a rock and their tongue sticks to it, it could be because it's fossilized bone! Bones are full of tiny holes, giving them a rough texture that a tongue sticks to.

Rock-licking is less popular than it used to be, because rock identification tools have become better, smaller, and cheaper. We also know that some rocks can be dangerous to lick—such as galena, which contains toxic **lead**!

MY TONGUE IS GETTING TIRED!

ITSH SHTUCK!

SWIMMING IN SYRUP

Do you think you could swim faster in water or syrup? Well, you can keep your syrup for pancakes, because two scientists have already done the hard work of finding out! They filled a pool with a syrup-like liquid and timed 16 volunteers swimming lengths of it.

The volunteers also swam lengths of a typical water-filled pool, and the scientists compared the results. They found that the swimmers went just as fast in the syrup as in the water! In the syrup, a swimmer experiences more drag (pushing-back force from the liquid) but the syrup's greater thickness also made each stroke produce more forward force.

These two effects cancel each other out, so overall it's similar to swimming in water. Although this science may sound silly, it actually helps us better answer important questions about how forces work in liquids. Super-famous scientist Isaac Newton wrote about this—how the thickness of a liquid might affect an object's speed through it. He never filled a pool with syrup, though!

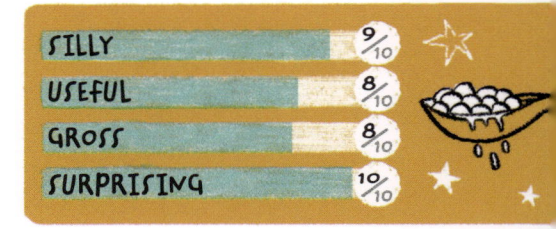

SILLY	9/10
USEFUL	8/10
GROSS	8/10
SURPRISING	10/10

LAST LENGTH, THEN YOU CAN HAVE A SHOWER!

To make the syrup, scientists mixed guar gum—an edible thickening agent—with water. The gum formed patches of snotty-looking scum on the top of the water. Mmmm, delicious!

UGGGHH . . . SO . . . STICKY!

Tip: This experiment will NOT work with floppy cooked spaghetti!

SNAPPING SPAGHETTI

With just a strand of dry spaghetti and a pair of protective goggles, you can do your very own Ig Nobel-inspired experiment! With your goggles on, simply hold the dry spaghetti strand at both ends and bend it until it snaps. What happens?

Your spaghetti broke into three or more pieces, right? This is what almost always happens, and it puzzled top scientists for decades because similarly hard, stick-like objects, such as pencils, typically break into two pieces.

Then new experiments showed that when a long, thin rod is strongly curved and released (like snapping spaghetti), a burst of powerful waves curves the rod even more before it becomes straight again. Wherever the curve is too intense, the spaghetti breaks so quickly that it looks like all the breaks happen at once.

It may seem silly, but this spaghetti study could save lives! It helps scientists understand how other long, **brittle** structures—from bridges to human bones—may break apart.

SILLY	8/10
USEFUL	4/10
GROSS	6/10
SURPRISING	2/10

SOGGY CEREAL

Do you hate when your favorite crunchy breakfast cereal goes all mushy before you've had a chance to finish it? Well, scientists haven't quite solved this sad, soggy problem yet, but they have used some pretty hi-tech equipment to learn more about how and why it happens!

I'M ALMOST READY FOR SCHOOL, I JUST NEED TO FINISH MY EXPERIMENT FIRST!

Scientists in the UK explored how contact with liquid affects the crunchiness of breakfast cereal flakes. After soaking some flakes in water for different lengths of time, they squashed them inside a machine designed to apply force in a steady, accurately measurable way. Then they used another machine to measure how much liquid the cereal flakes contained.

The scientists discovered that a flake can take on a certain amount of liquid while staying crunchy. Beyond this point, it's a downhill journey to sogginess, with a particularly speedy change as the flake's water content grows from 12% to 18%.

The scientists' experiments used water rather than milk. Although milk should give roughly the same results, perhaps someone—maybe you?—should double-check!

TUMBLING TOAST

Have you ever noticed that if you drop a piece of toast, it almost always seems to fall butter-side down on the floor? "WHY??!" you might be wondering, as you sadly pick up your ruined, fluff-covered toast.

You might expect that, like when you toss a coin in the air, a slice of toast has a 50% chance of landing on either side. However, scientist Robert Matthews realized that, unlike coins, toast typically falls on the floor after sliding off a plate on a table or in someone's hand, not after being thrown up in the air.

As toast sits on a plate butter-side up, Matthews worked out that at this lower height it doesn't have time to spin all the way round. It only manages a half-turn, if anything, so the buttered side is more likely to end up face down and landing on the floor.

SILLY 8/10
USEFUL 4/10
GROSS 7/10
SURPRISING 8/10

More than 1,000 children took part in a 2001 experiment to put Matthews' theory to the test. The toast fell butter-side down off a plate around 6 out of 10 times!

ARGH, MY TOAST!

SILLY		6/10
USEFUL		8/10
GROSS		8/10
SURPRISING		7/10

FIVE-SECOND RULE

You may have heard someone shout "Five-second rule!" when their food falls on the floor, just before they pick it up and eat it. Maybe you've even done this yourself? The thinking is that it takes time for bacteria to move on to your dropped food, so you can still safely eat it as long as you grab it quickly enough.

When Jillian Clarke was a high-school student, she won an Ig Nobel prize for what seems to be the first research into the five-second rule. While at a special university program, she covered floor tiles with bacteria and placed food items on the tiles for varying lengths of time. The bacteria did transfer oto at least some of the foods—including a cookie and a gummy bear candy—within 5 seconds. And that's bad news for food-droppers everywhere!

IT'S HARD TO RUN ON CARPET!

INCOMING! GO! GO! GO!

While the five-second rule is generally untrue, scientists have found that some things affect how quickly bacteria can transfer. They include the type of food dropped, and the material and dirtiness of the floor.

ARGHHHHH!

SLIPPING ON A BANANA PEEL

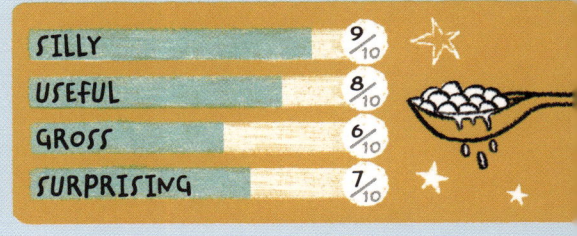

SILLY		9/10
USEFUL		8/10
GROSS		6/10
SURPRISING		7/10

You may have seen cartoon characters slip on banana peels and then crash dramatically to the floor. But are banana peels actually that slippery? A team of scientists in Japan ran experiments to find out!

One of the scientists stepped on a banana peel placed on top of a piece of **linoleum** flooring. The flooring was fixed on to equipment designed to measure different forces, including **friction**.

The friction between the banana peel and the flooring was around six times less than that of the shoe on the flooring. This meant the banana peel was six times more slippery than the floor.

The scientists believe this is largely because cells on the inside of banana peels ooze slippery mucus (a thick snot-like liquid) when they are stepped on!

This research has helped scientists understand how mucus helps keep joints (where bones meet) moving smoothly. It may help us design better artificial joints for humans.

QUIZ TIME!

1. What could experiments on slippery banana peels help scientists to design?

2. Which animal's poop is key to the world's most expensive coffee?

3. Why is a piece of toast more likely to land butter-side down?

4. If you bend a strand of spaghetti until it snaps, does it usually break in two?

5. If a scientist licks a rock and their tongue sticks to it, what could this mean?

6. Does bacteria always take more than five seconds to transfer on to dropped food?

7. How much more milk per year do cows with names produce?

8. Do you swim a lot slower in syrup than in water?

9. If a cookie is coated on one side with chocolate, can you dunk it for longer?

10. How can chewing gum be used to solve crimes?

NOW CHECK YOUR ANSWERS ON PAGE 80. HOW DID YOU DO?

DO YOU MIND?

The human brain may be clever, but it can still be tricked! Scientists are always looking for new ways to discover how we really think.

THE INVISIBLE GORILLA

If you were watching a video of a few people playing basketball and someone in a gorilla costume wandered through the game, do you think you'd notice? What if the gorilla stopped right in the middle of the screen, looked straight at you and beat its chest with its hands? According to an experiment from 1999, HALF of the volunteers who watched this video didn't see the gorilla at all!

What the scientists were testing was something called inattentional blindness. Basically, it means that when you're concentrating hard on looking at one particular thing, your brain can sometimes ignore other things that are also visible. Even a gorilla!

You could ask an adult to search online for the original video from the experiment. You'll probably notice the gorilla because you're expecting it, but try it out on a friend or family member!

SILLY		9/10
USEFUL		8/10
GROSS		1/10
SURPRISING		10/10

Researching inattentional blindness can help in important areas such as road safety. Studies have found that drivers using cell phones (even hands-free) miss up to 50% of what's going on around them, causing them to make dangerous mistakes.

The volunteers in this experiment were asked to count how many times the players in white passed the basketball. This was quite tricky because players dressed in black were also passing around a basketball, and all the players were moving around.

The volunteers were then asked how many passes they counted—and if they'd seen the gorilla. Around half were shocked by the question. They were so busy concentrating on the white team's passes that they hadn't noticed the gorilla at all!

Other scientists have created videos with someone in a gorilla costume moving at different speeds. They found that volunteers were more likely to see a faster-moving gorilla. This could be because the human brain sees a speedier, unexpected object as more of a threat, and so less safe to ignore.

TAP
TAP

SOUND RAGE

TAP TAP TAP. COUGH COUGH COUGH. CHEW CHEW CHEW. It can be annoying, and sometimes kind of gross, to have to listen to the various bodily noises of other people around you. Is there a particular "human sound" that makes you cringe?

This slight annoyance or disgust is totally normal, but when people feel it to the extreme it's known as misophonia—otherwise known as "sound rage." People with misophonia can get so riled up that they have to leave the room if someone starts sniffing, biting their nails, or eating a bag of potato chips!

A trio of Dutch scientists won an Ig Nobel Prize for their research arguing that misophonia is a real mental health condition. They found that people with misophonia don't want to be grumpy about others making typical human sounds —they know it would be unreasonable to expect them not to! So they often find ways to cope, from putting on music or distracting themselves with a task to avoiding certain places where they're likely to hear their most-hated noises.

WILL YOU ALL BE

QUIET?!

Other common sounds that people with misophonia can struggle with hearing are sneezing, swallowing, footsteps, typing, pen clicking, and loud breathing.

SNIFF

CRUNCH!

TAP TAP

ITCH-SCRATCHING PLEASURE

As annoying as an itch can be, scratching it in just the right spot can feel pretty good! But just how good? That's what a team of scientists set up an experiment to try to find out.

First, they rubbed each volunteer's ankle, forearm and back with sharp hairs from the tropical cowhage plant, known to cause severe itchiness. They then used a thin brush to scratch the now-itchy areas. Throughout the experiment—every 30 seconds over a total of 5 minutes—the volunteers were asked how intense the itching felt and how pleasurable the scratching felt.

The scientists found that how long itching lasts and how intense it feels, as well as how much scratching helps stop itching and how pleasurable it feels, seems to vary across our body. For example, on the forearm and ankle—but not the back—a more intense itch also meant a more pleasurable scratch.

SILLY	8/10
USEFUL	3/10
GROSS	7/10
SURPRISING	7/10

YES, THAT'S THE SPOT!

Scientists asked volunteers to use the Visual Analog Scale to score how intense their itches felt and how pleasurable the scratching felt. This scale is typically used to measure pain, from 0 (no pain) to 10 (the worst pain imaginable).

NEEDLESSLY LONG WORDS

You might think that using as many long, complicated, sophisticated, intricate, elaborate, extensive, protracted (you get the picture!) words as possible in your writing would make it seem better. After all, it shows off how many words you know, right?

Professor Daniel Oppenheimer had noticed that some of his students seemed to deliberately use more complicated words than they needed to in their writing. Some research appeared to support this idea, with four out of five students admitting to swapping more complex language into their writing to try to sound more intelligent.

Although there's no problem at all with using long words, deliberately avoiding shorter words goes against writing experts' advice to write as simply and clearly as possible. Oppenheimer set up experiments where he asked people to compare writing samples that used either a straightforward style or a complex one to give the same information. He found that the more the writing included needlessly long words, the worse people tended to think it was!

The title of Daniel Oppenheimer's research paper is "Consequences of Erudite Vernacular Utilized Irrespective of Necessity." A little joke about using needlessly long words!

EXIT →

HMPH! SURELY THE SIGN SHOULD READ, "YOUR AVENUE OF EGRESS IS IN THE DIRECTION INDICATED"?!

SILLY 7/10
USEFUL 8/10
GROSS 1/10
SURPRISING 8/10

SILLY 5/10
USEFUL 7/10
GROSS 1/10
SURPRISING 9/10

DON'T YOU JUST LOOOVE THIS PIRATE METAL COUNTRY-PUNK MUSIC FUSION?!

HUH??!!

DO YOU MIND?

THE POWER OF "HUH?"

You may not have thought much about "Huh?"—a short word that we use when we haven't heard or understood what someone has said. But, amazingly, researchers believe that this little word is universal—meaning that it exists in every spoken human language in the world!

Rather than trying to study all of these 7,000 or so languages, the researchers listened to recordings of real conversations in ten languages. These languages came from a diverse range of language families (groups of languages that work in similar ways).

They found that across these different languages, "Huh?" may be spelled and pronounced a bit differently, but the general sound and use of the word is almost exactly the same. Most words vary massively across different language families—for example, the English word "dog" sounds very different to the Japanese word ("inu") and the French one ("chien").

HUH??

"Huh?" is an important word because it gives us a way to tell someone when we haven't understood what they've said. This helps keep conversations on track and avoid misunderstandings.

MIRROR ITCHES

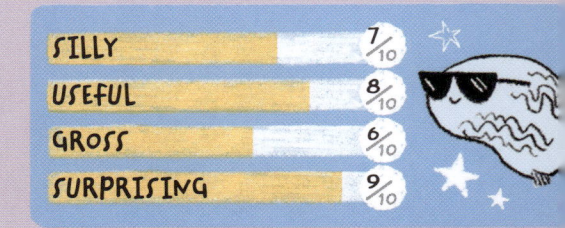

The urge to scratch an itch can be almost impossible to resist, even when you know it'll make things worse! Scratching eczema, chicken pox, and insect bites can damage your skin, but (ooh, just a quick scratch) the itchiness they cause (come on, one scratch won't hurt, right?!) can (go on, SCRAATCH!) make it hard to think of anything else.

Scientists may have found a solution to this itchy issue, though—using only a mirror and someone to help! They set up an experiment in which they first injected volunteers with a substance called histamine in their right arm to make it feel itchy. They then scratched either the volunteers' left or right arms with a metal strip. Unsurprisingly, the volunteers said that only scratching the itchy right arm relieved the itch.

The histamine injection caused a red mark to form on each volunteer's right arm. The scientists painted a red mark on the other arm so the volunteers couldn't tell which was the itchy arm just by looking!

Real itch

Fake itch

66

THAT HELPS A BIT . . . BUT IT'S STILL SORTA ITCHY!

Real itch

Fake itch

The scientists then set up a mirror blocking this itchy arm. They asked the volunteers to only look at the arm reflected in the mirror.

When this non-itchy left arm was scratched, the mirror made it look like the right one, and it helped relieve the itch! Only about a quarter as much as scratching the itchy arm, but it still seemed to show that our brain can override other messages from our body when they mismatch with what we see.

The scientists also set up a similar experiment using video screens blocking the volunteers' arms. They played real-time videos showing the volunteers' arms being scratched, sometimes flipping the video so it looked like the opposite arm was being scratched. Just as with the mirror experiment, the volunteers felt some relief when the non-itchy arm was scratched, but only if it looked like it was the itchy arm.

The scientists hope that "mirror scratching" could give some relief to people who suffer from long-term itching and often scratch their skin until it bleeds. This break could also help their skin to recover.

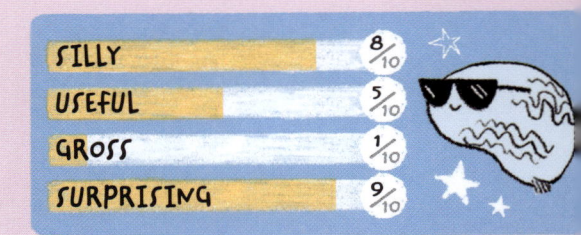

SHRINKING THE EIFFEL TOWER

The Eiffel Tower in Paris, France is one of the most famous buildings in the world. It stands around 985 feet (300 meters) tall—about as high as 100 elephants standing on each other's backs. But scientists have found a way to make the Eiffel Tower seem smaller—just lean to the left!

In a study of 33 people, those who leaned to the left while guessing the height of the Eiffel Tower typically thought it was about 40 feet (12 meters) shorter than those who stood upright or leaned to the right. None of the volunteers knew what its actual height was, so they were always just guessing.

The volunteers didn't realize that they were leaning at all. They had been asked to stand up straight on an electronic balance board, lining themselves up with guide marks on a linked screen. But these marks had actually been changed so when it said the volunteers were upright, they were sometimes unknowingly leaning slightly to the left or right!

1 2 3 4 5 6 7 8 9 10

The reason behind this odd result may be linked to the "mental number line" theory. Apparently, people typically imagine numbers on a horizontal line, with smaller numbers on the left and larger ones on the right.

ARGHH!

ERRM . . . 820 FEET TALL?

780 FEET TALL?

OOH, IT'S ALL UPSIDE-DOWNY!

SILLY	9/10
USEFUL	4/10
GROSS	3/10
SURPRISING	8/10

LOOKING THROUGH YOUR LEGS

If you bend over and gaze out at the world through your legs, it will look pretty different to how you see it when you're upright. And not just because it's upside-down!

Professors Atsuki Higashiyama and Kohei Adachi set up an experiment in which they asked volunteers to look at five red rectangles of different sizes, placed at different distances from them. Each volunteer was asked how big and how far away each target seemed.

Some volunteers stood upright, while others bent over and looked through their legs. Some stood upright but wore special prism goggles that made the world look flipped upside-down. And others wore these goggles while looking through their legs, so things actually looked the right way round!

When people looked through their legs, even if they were wearing the goggles, they judged the objects to be farther away than they actually were . . . at least, for distances up to 50 feet (15 meters). It seems that their body position—not just their eyes' upside-down view—affected how their brain saw the world.

DO YOU MIND?

Flip the page!

TELLING TWINS APART

Some identical twins look so similar that even their parents struggle to tell them apart. Now, scientists have found that identical twins often can't tell themselves apart either!

In an experiment in Italy, ten pairs of identical twins were each joined by a relative or close friend of the twins. As far as possible, this person looked similar to the twins. The twins and the relative/close friend were each shown a number of photos—of themselves and the two others. Some of these photos were upright and some were upside-down.

They were asked to identify, as quickly as possible, who was in each picture. The twins typically knew when a photo was of their relative/close friend, but often found it difficult to know if a photo showed themselves or their twin! This was especially true when the photo was upside-down. In fact, they were no better at telling themselves apart than their relative/close friend was!

Around 1 in 250 births are of identical twins. This happens when a single fertilized egg splits in two, creating two people who share the same **genes**.

THAT'S ME, RIGHT? NO, IT'S YOU!

I THOUGHT WE KNEW WHO WE WERE?!

SILLY	7/10 ★
USEFUL	5/10
GROSS	1/10
SURPRISING	8/10 ☆

LOOK UP!

Back in 1968, on a busy street in New York City, 15 people stood staring up at a building's fifth-floor window. Most people who passed them looked up at the window too, and almost half of them stopped to properly stare at it. After a minute, the original 15 people wandered off. So, what was so interesting about that window?

Nothing at all! It was part of an experiment to see how people responded to a crowd of up to 15 people, or even a single person, looking up at something for 60 seconds.

Just one person looking up made 42 in 100 of the people passing do the same, but only 4 in 100 actually stopped to look. A bigger crowd led to a bigger effect on passersby. A whopping 86 in 100 people looked up when a 15-person crowd did, with 40 in 100 people stopping to stare up at nothing!

The scientists recorded videos of the 50-foot (15-meter) length of the street where the experiment took place. Afterward, they watched the videos back and counted all the passersby and how they reacted—must have taken ages!

ANNOYING ALARM CLOCK

Do you ever have trouble getting out of bed in the morning? When inventor Gauri Nanda was a university student, she did too. She would often sleepily hit the snooze button on her alarm clock again and again, ending up oversleeping and being late to her morning classes.

One morning, she realized—her alarm clock was the problem. So, as a project for her design class, she created a furry alarm clock with wheels that you had to chase around the bedroom to turn off! Some popular tech websites featured her invention and it went viral. So many people wanted one that she spent two years developing it as a (non-furry) product, calling it Clocky.

When Clocky's loud alarm goes off, it leaps from your nightstand and races around the room. It hides in different places, forcing you to get up to stop the annoying beeping. Clocky-chasing should wake you up enough that you don't just fall back asleep!

SILLY	8/10	★ ★
USEFUL	9/10	
GROSS	1/10	
SURPRISING	8/10	☆

Speech bubbles: "I KNOW HOW TO SPELL "TOMATO" . . ." "... SO WHY DOES "TOMATO TOMATO TOMATO TOMATO" LOOK WEIRD?"

WORD-REPEATING WEIRDNESS

SILLY	7/10
USEFUL	6/10
GROSS	5/10
SURPRISING	7/10

Have you ever said, read, or written a word over and over again, and noticed that it makes you feel a bit weird? Like the word doesn't sound or look right—or maybe doesn't even seem like a real word any more?!

Scientists have called this feeling "jamais vu," which is French for "never seen." It describes the way that familiar words start to feel strangely unfamiliar when we say, read, or write them lots of times in a row. Sometimes they lose meaning and just seem like a string of random letters.

An Ig Nobel prize-winning research team found that this starts to happen after people write the same word around 30 times, or after about a minute. This effect only seems to affect two out of three people, though.

"Jamais vu" appears more likely to happen with words that we use either quite often or very often. It is a lot rarer with words that are less familiar to us in the first place.

PUZZLE-SOLVING SLIME MOLDS

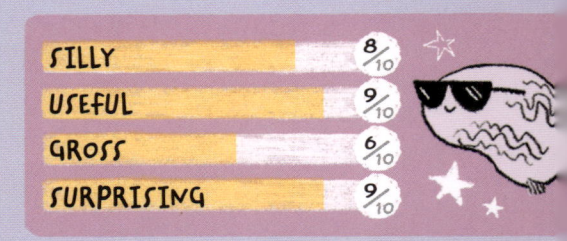

Slime molds are amazingly bizarre life forms that are neither animals, plants, nor **fungi**. They belong to a mish-mash group of living things called **protists**, which also includes algae.

Although slime molds don't have brains, they show unexpected signs of intelligence. Scientists in Japan found that a plasmodial slime mold could find the shortest route through a maze!

WELCOME TO THE SLIME MOLD MAZE RACE!

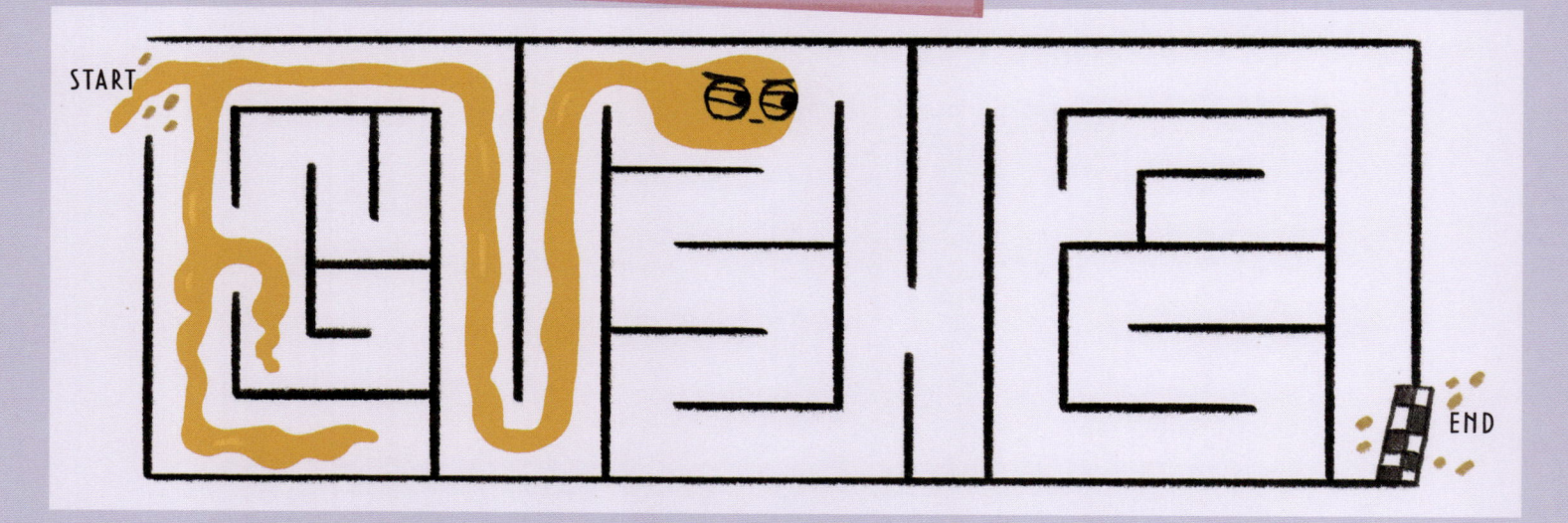

The slime mold spread out through the maze in search of food. The maze had oat flakes—which slime molds seem to like eating—at its start and end.

YOU CAN DO THIS, SYD SLIME!

GO GET THOSE OATS!

Many living things—including plants, fungi, bacteria, coral, and jellyfish—don't have a brain. Scientists are learning more about the different ways these life forms can use information to help them survive.

8 HOURS LATER . . .

START

END

When the slime mold found the food at the maze's end, it pulled back from the dead ends and longer possible routes, letting the parts of itself left there decay. The remaining slime mold formed the shortest path between the two food sources. All in all, the slime mold took around 8 hours to solve the puzzle.

WOOOOHOOOO!

YOU'RE OUR HERO, SYD SLIME!

While a slime mold is one single cell, your body is made up of about 17 TRILLION cells.

Slime molds' ability to find the most efficient routes could help us plan transport networks. In other experiments, scientists used food to represent cities and slime molds then recreated maps of road and railway lines between them.

SLI'ME A GENIUS!

QUIz TIME!

1   Does leaning to the left or the right make the Eiffel Tower look smaller?

2   What is misophonia?

3   Which plant did scientists rub on people's skin to make them itchy, to test how nice it felt to then scratch that itch?

4   Can identical twins always tell themselves apart, even if no one else can?

5   What word seems to exist in every language in the world?

6   What feeling does the term "jamais vu" describe?

7   Does using unnecessarily long words make your writing seem better or worse?

8   What does the term "inattentional blindness" mean?

9   What group of living things does a slime mold belong to?

10 How many people, out of 100, stopped to look up at nothing just because a group of 15 people did?

NOW CHECK YOUR ANSWERS ON PAGE 80. HOW DID YOU DO?

CONCLUSION

Now you're a science expert who can spot an "invisible" gorilla and knows how to dunk a cookie scientifically! But which of these scientific discoveries surprised you the most?

Which one was so gross, you nearly lost your lunch?

And, most importantly, which one was your overall favorite?

We've almost reached the end of the book, and you've probably learned more about stinky feet and various types of animal poop than you ever wanted to know. You're welcome!

But hopefully between disbelieving "Nooooooo"s and disgusted "Eeewwwww"s, you've seen the ways that silly-seeming science can actually teach us really important things about our world. Sometimes, it can change—or even save—lives!

There are all kinds of ways to understand our world better, and you never know where curiosity can lead to. Could studying slug slime hold the key to curing all diseases? Could measuring the scream factor of roller coasters uncover a secret force of nature? Who knows! But scientists could learn a lot along the way—and have a lot of fun too.

GLOSSARY

Analysis/analyze
Careful, detailed study of something to better understand what it is and how it works.

Apparatus
A set of equipment or tools for a particular use.

Artificial
Not natural, made by people.

Bacteria
Tiny, often single-celled living things that can sometimes cause diseases.

Brittle
Hard but fragile and easily broken.

Carbohydrate
A natural substance, such as a starch or a sugar, that gives the body energy. Foods such as bread, rice, and fruit are sources of carbohydrates.

Electromagnet
A type of magnet, in which an electric current is passed through wire wrapped around a piece of iron or steel. The electricity makes it magnetic.

Extract
To separate out and remove something.

Fatty acids
A type of acid naturally contained in vegetable and animal fats and oils.

Filter
A device that removes something unwanted from a gas or liquid as it passes through.

Force
A push or pull in a particular direction, acting on an object.

Fossil
The remains or imprint, in the ground or rock, of a living thing from a long time ago.

Friction
A rubbing force between two objects that are moving past each other. It makes them move less quickly and smoothly.

Fungi
A fungus (plural: fungi) is a type of living thing. It usually lives on plants or dead, decaying matter.

Galaxy
A huge system that includes billions of stars, gas, and other matter, held together by gravity.

Genes
Information in the cells of our body, passed down to us from our parents. Genes can affect what we look like and how we behave.

Immune
Protected against a particular disease, either naturally or because of having a vaccination.

Infra-red
A type of light wave that is too long for humans to see, but that we can feel as heat. Infra-red cameras help us detect hot or cold objects.

Intestine
A long, winding, tube-like organ that can form the lower part of an animal's (and a human's) digestive system, below the stomach.

Lead
A soft, heavy, poisonous gray metal.

Linoleum
A smooth, waterproof material often used to cover kitchen and bathroom floors. It is made by pressing ground-up wood and oil onto cloth.

Marsupial
An animal such as a kangaroo, wallaby, or wombat. The female marsupial has a pouch on her front, in which she carries her baby after it is born.

Mineral
A solid, pure substance that forms naturally in the ground and doesn't come from a plant or animal.

Molecule
A tiny particle made of one or more atoms, which are the universe's basic building blocks. It is the smallest unit of a substance, such as water, that still has all the features of that substance.

Navigate
To find the right direction to travel by using maps, equipment, or natural landmarks.

Organ
A part of the body, such as the heart or lungs, that performs a particular job.

Parasite
A living thing that can only survive by getting food and energy from a host, another living thing that is typically harmed by this.

Petri dish
A round, shallow, see-through glass or plastic dish, often used for growing bacteria.

Professor
An expert teacher at a university or college.

Protein
A natural substance that your body needs to grow and repair itself. Foods such as eggs, meat, and beans are good sources of protein.

Protist
A type of living thing that doesn't fit into the animal, plant, fungi, or bacteria groups. Protists are usually so small that you need a microscope to see them.

Satellite
A machine launched into space to travel around Earth. It often collects information, such as weather patterns, or helps to make communication systems (such as TV, phones, and radio) work.

Smart
Describes a device, such as a phone or watch, that is connected to the internet and uses digital technology.

Study
An experiment or piece of research that scientists do to learn more about something. They write down what they did, and what their results were, to share with others.

Supplement
A special pill or food that you take or eat regularly to help improve your health.

Territory
An area that an animal has claimed as its own, and typically marked in some way to let other animals of its kind know to stay away.

Water vapor
Water in the form of a gas, but typically cooler than steam (water above its boiling point of roughly 212 °F (100 °C).

ANSWERS

ANIMAL ANTICS (PAGE 26)

1. It makes it easier to swim.
2. A cube—half-point if you said square!
3. He cut out a pair of cardboard cat paws and walked them over a computer keyboard!
4. Any three of the following: Frog, strawberry, hazelnut, cherry tomato, fish, grasshopper, mouse.
5. Any of the following: Pablo Picasso, Claude Monet, Paul Cézanne, Georges Braque.
6. The white polar bear disguise!
7. Some types of herring.
8. To check whether the whale has any serious diseases.
9. They put tiny cardboard hats on the beetles.
10. A dog flea! It jumps, on average, 1 inch (2.3 cm) higher than a cat flea.

ODD BOD (PAGE 42)

1. Apply force to the hoop in both a forward/backward and up/down direction, at the same time.
2. Yes! Maybe from growing, maybe from sagging.
3. Limburger cheese.
4. Any of the following: pee-testing strips, sensors that record when and how long someone is on the toilet, a camera that can identify someone by their butt, and a poop-checking computer system.
5. 4.5%—if you said anything between 1% and 10%, have a half-point.
6. Lactase.
7. Foot odor.
8. More comfortable—but still very uncomfortable!
9. Copper.
10. Activated charcoal.

ALL IN GOOD TASTE (PAGE 58)

1. Better artificial joints for humans.
2. A luwak, or palm civet.
3. Because it typically starts out butter-side up and falls from quite a low height, so only has time to turn once before it hits the ground.
4. No, it almost always breaks into three or more pieces.
5. That part of the rock could be fossilized bone.
6. No, it often takes much less than 5 seconds.
7. Around 55 gallons (250 liters, or 1,000 glasses) of milk.
8. No, it's about the same time overall.
9. Yes, especially if you do a "scientific dunk" with the chocolatey side facing upward.
10. Bacteria from a gum-chewing criminal's mouth could be analyzed and identified.

DO YOU MIND? (PAGE 76)

1. To the left.
2. "Sound rage"—when people find certain sounds so annoying, it makes them feel angry, disgusted, or physically uncomfortable.
3. The tropical cowhage plant.
4. No! In a study, they did no better than a close friend or family member.
5. Huh?
6. The way that familiar words start to feel strangely unfamiliar when we say or write them lots of times in a row.
7. Worse, according to a scientific study.
8. When you're concentrating so hard on looking at one particular thing that your brain ignores other things that you can also see.
9. Protists.
10. A whopping 86 out of 100 people, in a study performed in 1968.

 There were 14 paper planes throughout the book! They're on pages 12, 15, 21, 25, 31, 35, 40, 44, 49, 51, 57, 65, 69, and 72.